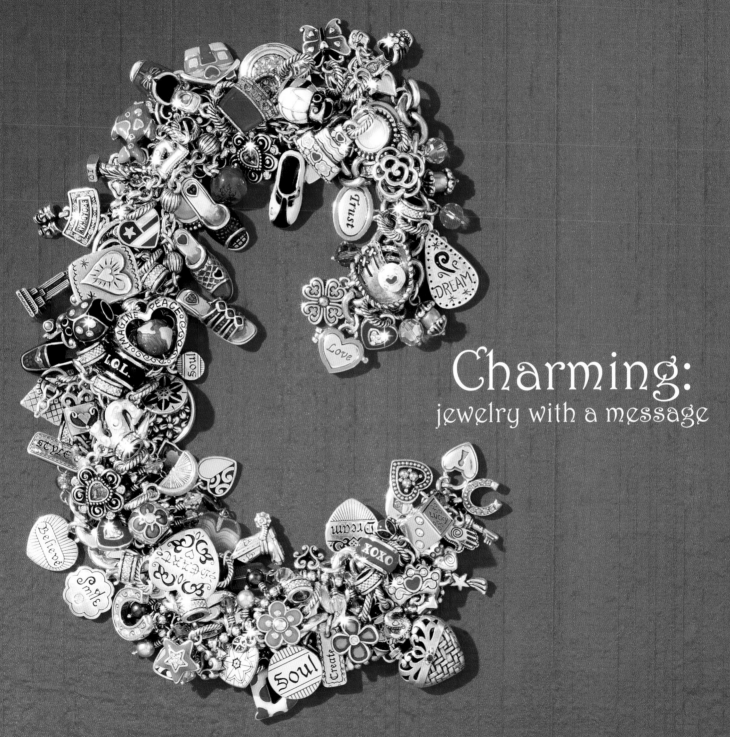

Charming:
jewelry with a message

PROJECT EDITOR: LORI MCFADDEN ♥ PHOTOGRAPHY: BRIAN GOODMAN AND KEVIN FOLEY ♥ WRITER: PHYLLIS HANSEN

foreward

By Jerry Kohl, Founder of Brighton Collectibles

Long before bling and glitz, and as far back as man or woman can recall, jewelry had a purpose. It carried messages. Native peoples embedded them with hieroglyphics. Eons passed and movie idols like Frank Sinatra figured out jewelry could sweet-talk a poker buddy like Marlene Dietrich. Even later, mid-century teens got the word out about the Fab Four concerts via their Beatles charm bracelets. Remember?

And what about you? There was that first seashell you pulled from the sand, hung on a string and gave to Mom -- a charm that said "I Love You" without a word spoken. Same for the class ring worn round your neck that told the world you were "going steady" …a charm in its own way. Messages can offer serious sentiments like hope and blessings or spark nostalgia, but by nature charm jewelry sends its messages with fun and wit. Think about it–a miraculously detailed miniature that swings, twirls, jingles and keeps you coming back for more is going to make you smile.

At Brighton, our designers are turning out silent messages at a more-the-merrier pace. Charms for best friends forever, lockets to keep your dog Betsy's "mug shot" close to your heart, tiny trinkets that magically open to reveal an even tinier surprise within. We're doing charms to use as bookmarks and zipper pulls and some to tie on shoe laces. Don't be surprised if they say hi to a stranger on your behalf. Charm messages are a little like texting, only better.

TABLE OF CONTENTS

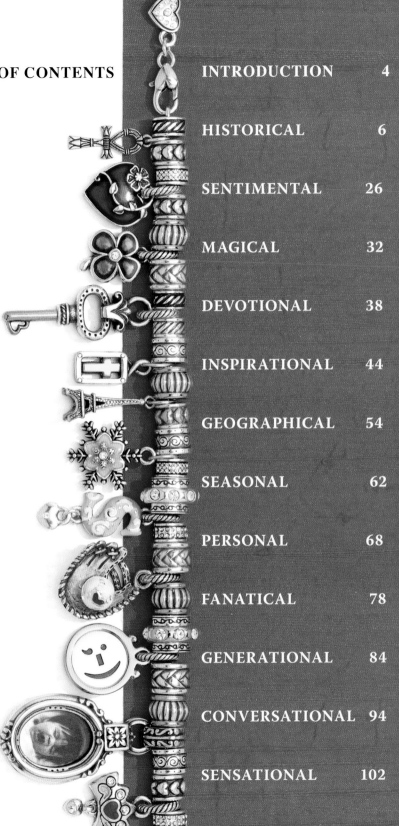

We designed this book to be sold in stores where Brighton is sold, where books are sold, or your favorite gift shop. $5 from the sale of each book will be donated to programs teaching jewelry making.

Creative contributors: Beth Barror, Tom Clancy, Maryam Nassirbegli, Mavis Peterson, Peggy Reed

First published in 2009 in hardcover in the United States of America by Brighton Collectibles, Inc. 14022 Nelson Avenue, City of Industry, CA 91746 www.brighton.com

Library of Congress Control Number: 2008941751

ISBN-978-1-932802-51-1

Printed in Hong Kong

Dear Rachel,

Today is a big day for you - one that you will remember all your life. (Your dad and I will, too!) Nothing is more precious than family, and now you and your new husband Nick will be starting your own. When your dad and I first met back in college, he bought me a charm bracelet that began with a single charm - a heart.

When we married, we added the wedding bells, and when you were born, your birthstone and the cutest baby shoes. The charms we've collected over the years mean so much...it's the journey of our life as a family.

And speaking of journeys, we could relive our family trips with these charms. (One was imaginary, to Oz ... you always loved Dorothy.)

From your 1st day of school when you brought the teacher an apple ...to dance class, soccer, graduation ... how did the time pass so quickly?

I bought this butterfly when you moved out on your own...to remind myself that a good mom is happy to see her daughter spread her wings.

Now your dreams have taken flight. Please take this bracelet as the "something old" to begin your own marriage. Add new charms, then pass it on to a daughter you may have one day, as our journey continues through the generations.

Love,
MOM

4

Since the dawn of civilization, people have coveted charms and amulets. Early on, a charm served as a guardian. Over time, charms became a means to connect with the divine. It was the ancient Egyptians who were first known to craft them into jewelry, using color and design to uplift, protect and invoke magical powers. During the middle ages, knights went to battle with lucky charms from their ladyloves dangling from their armor. (Just imagine the jingling!) Not to be outdone, kings of olde found charms useful for curses on the enemy (re-visited today in electronic gameplay.) In the first voyages to America, legend has it the Dutch traded their beads, trinkets and mirrored objets d'art with the native people in return for safe haven on the island of Manhattan. Noble or bewitching, sacred or profane, the ancient talismans still tell tales. The fascination with the miniature links us all. It just might be part of our DNA.

Treasure of Khnumet, an Egyptian princess's openwork collar circa 1895 b.c. Known as weskhats with leaf-shaped pendants strung between horizontal rows, they are said to be favorites of gods and pharaohs alike.

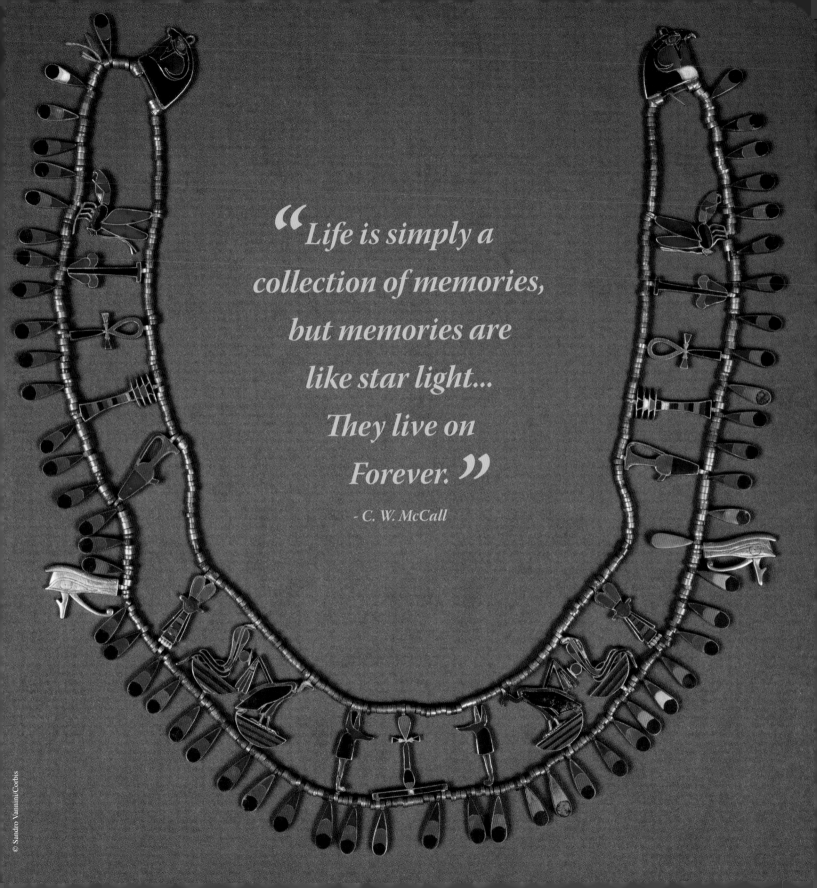

"Life is simply a collection of memories, but memories are like star light... They live on Forever.

- C. W. McCall

It would seem the crown jewels weren't enough for a sentimental sort like Queen Victoria. Among this famous monarch's long list of legacies is her penchant for decorative accessories that we know as Victoriana. A jewelry buff of the first order, she layered on necklaces and pendants, popularized chatelaines and even had a charm bracelet or two up her sleeve. Mad for these bracelets, one of her most notable dangled lockets with portrait miniatures of her children. Another supposedly memorialized their baby teeth. When her beloved Prince Albert died before his time, causing Victoria to adopt permanent mourning status, yet another elaborate jewelry trend rippled across England and the former Colonies. Her passion for black mourning jewelry caught on. Now a century later, give or take, this Queen's influence as the world's most trendsetting widow shows no sign of abating. Collectors still prize the real thing while modern designers find endless inspiration in Victoriana. Now, it's just been noted by royal-watchers that Victoria's great-great granddaughter, Her Majesty Queen Elizabeth II, has inherited this love for good luck charms. She is said to carry an amazing array of miniature horses, dogs, saddles and such gifted to her by her family.

Long live the queens and their charms!

9

isn't it romantic?

Victoriana then, Victoriana now. These little charmers play history-on-a-wrist in encore performances for the neo-romantic.

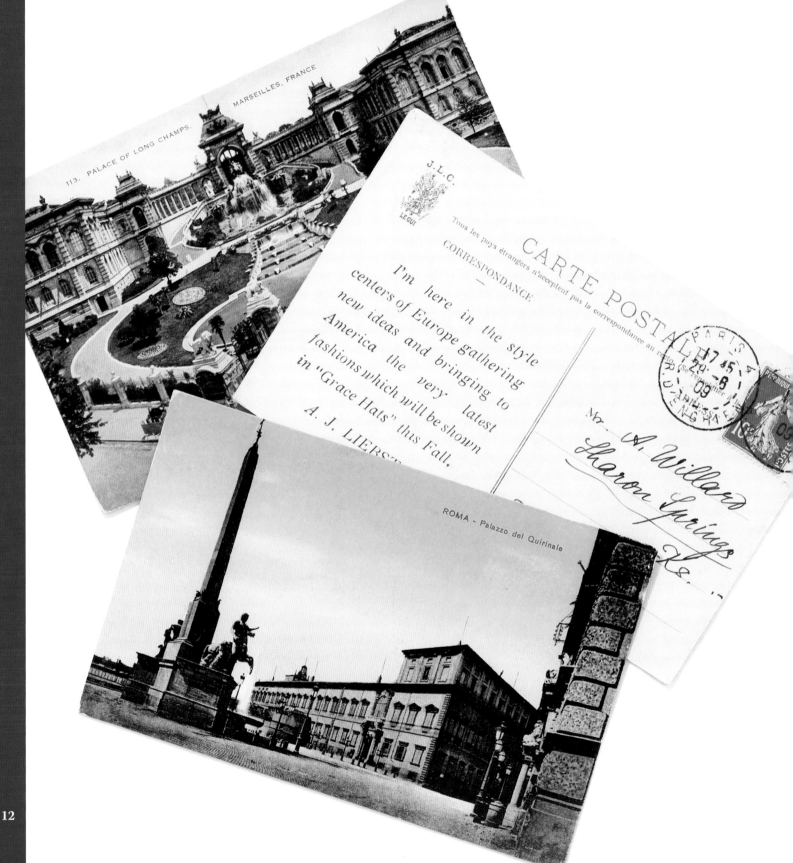

MARSEILLES, FRANCE

113. PALACE OF LONG CHAMPS.

J.L.C.

LE GUI

CARTE POSTALE

Tous les pays étrangers n'acceptent pas la correspondance au recto (se renseigner à la poste)

CORRESPONDANCE

—

I'm here in the style centers of Europe gathering new ideas and bringing to America the very latest fashions which will be shown in "Grace Hats" this Fall.

A. J. LIERSE

PARIS

17 45

29 –B

09

Mr. A. Willard

Sharon Springs

ROMA - Palazzo del Quirinale

If you were a scholar in the 1600s, you might have been among the first to travel abroad on the Grand Tour. It was an arduous journey for a young man on a set itinerary to study Western Civilization in the capitals of Europe. By the late 19th century, people began making the trip for pleasure. Still on the prescribed Grand Tour path to see the ancient monuments, architecture, arts and culture, sojourns included London, Paris, Florence, Venice, and sometimes on to the East. Remember "Room with a View"? A trip could last a year, the idea of the tour paving the way for the modern vacationers of the next century. Europe was waiting with all her charms, including many miniature replicas to remember her by.

As mistress of the castle, or the chateau as it were, **the Chatelaine** was the keeper of the keys. As was the style in medieval times, she wore them swinging from fob chains or ribbons pinned to her waist. By the 18th century, sewing implements replaced keys, with scissors, thimbles, pincushions, tape measures and needle cases hung from the chatelaine, or "equipage". Notebooks, pencils, penknives and corkscrews soon joined this extravagant sewing party going on at the waist, and it became the Swiss Army Knife of its era. Circa 1880, chatelaines got dressed up in sterling silver, adding glorious Victorian extravagances like scent bottles and watches. Utilitarian chatelaines had morphed into charm-like jewelry, to remain until our short skirts and handbags bid them a fond adieu.

In 1928, Mexico lifted its passport requirement, and tourism south of the border was off and running. A pop culture fascination with all things Mexican followed in the ensuing decades. Colorful Bakelite jewelry, also new on the scene, captured the vibrancy and motifs perfectly while souvenir charms in sterling were a natural fit with Mexico's burgeoning silver jewelry industry.

In addition to one's prized charm jewelry, there were the toy "prizes" that turned up inside boxes of snacks. It's been quipped that these early celluloid treasures were so sought after that the treat itself was merely edible fill.

W

orked like a charm, American aviator Jacqueline Cochran seems to say, as she shows the lucky 13-charm bracelet she wouldn't leave home without. She is in London in 1941 following her historic transatlantic feat as the first woman to pilot a heavy bomber across the North Atlantic. In 1953, she was the first woman to break the sound barrier. Talk about breaking the proverbial glass ceilings!

19

It was the 1950s and "Everybody Liked Ike." First Lady Mamie Eisenhower thinks he's swell, too, judging by the IKE charm she wears when planning a fundraiser at the Waldorf-Astoria. The Fifties ushered in a brand new heydey for the iconic charm bracelet, and no matter if you were born with a silver spoon or were just plain folks, charm collecting was the thing to do. There was no better sign of these times than a memory book for the wrist. High society women took the bracelets to chic new levels, like the Oriental example here.

50s flashback

Let's all do the twist…or jitterbug the night away. Everything started rockin' and rollin' in the Fifties, and that included silver link bracelets chock full of charms. Why, the jangling charms could have made music on "American Bandstand" all on their own. More than a bracelet, it is a genuine conversation piece.

Just a spot of tea…and other very Eastern charms are clustered together, from the sampan to the Pagoda and an Asian character.

A very tiny mezuzah scroll charm hangs from its appointed link, to touch, bless, remind of the Torah.

An antique foreign coin with garland is turned into a lucky charm for the bracelet collection.

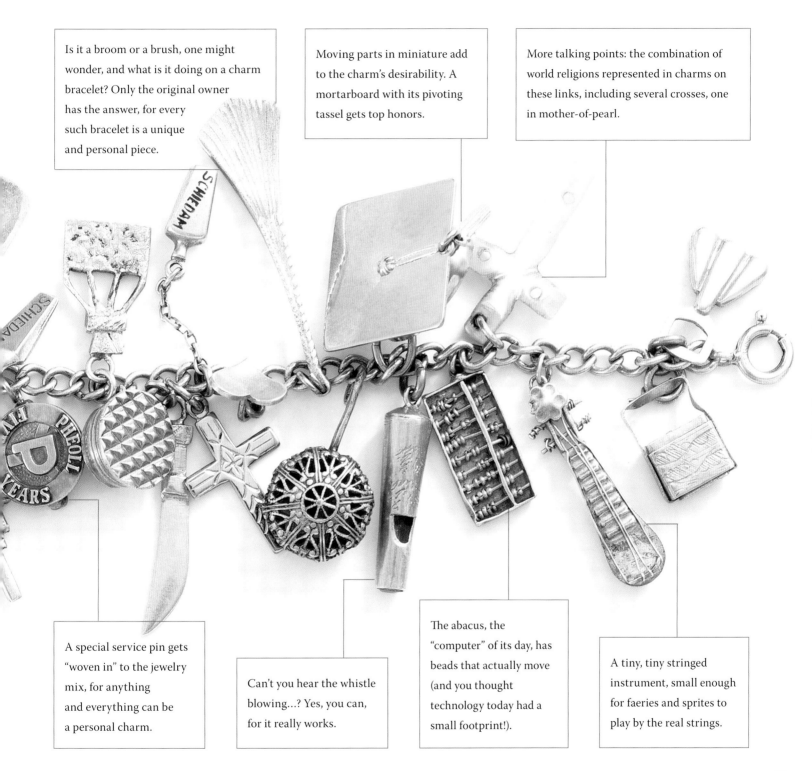

Is it a broom or a brush, one might wonder, and what is it doing on a charm bracelet? Only the original owner has the answer, for every such bracelet is a unique and personal piece.

Moving parts in miniature add to the charm's desirability. A mortarboard with its pivoting tassel gets top honors.

More talking points: the combination of world religions represented in charms on these links, including several crosses, one in mother-of-pearl.

A special service pin gets "woven in" to the jewelry mix, for anything and everything can be a personal charm.

Can't you hear the whistle blowing…? Yes, you can, for it really works.

The abacus, the "computer" of its day, has beads that actually move (and you thought technology today had a small footprint!).

A tiny, tiny stringed instrument, small enough for faeries and sprites to play by the real strings.

70s

80s

90s

What's your sign? Check the bracelet! There's a pretty good chance a 70s girl would have her zodiac symbol charm hanging from the links. Pirouetting mermaids were in vogue, as was the embedded mustard seed.

Miss GotRocks liked to flaunt these fun, chunky danglers in this oh so trendy decade. Lucite "ice cubes" and balls mingled with jumbo faux pearls and, as the Eighties got underway, looked great dancing under the disco ball.

Between 80s excess and 90s minimalism, it was off the wrist and onto the necklace with charms. Groups of charms were worn on chains, then the multiple chains layered round the neckline in graduated lengths.

"*Le coeur a ses raisons*
que la raison
ne connait point."

(The heart has reasons
the mind cannot know.)
--Pascal,
Pensées

25

> *Love to faults is always blind, blind,*
> *Always is to joy inclined,*
> *Lawless, winged and unconfined,*
> *And breaks all chains from every mind.*
>
> — William Blake

Eternal symbol of love, the heart has been precious throughout history. Once deemed to be the body's center of thought and intellect, and hence the source of one's soul, the connection to romance followed. Its fanciful scalloped shape endures, only to be tweaked, embellished, plumped, flourished, spliced and otherwise re-invented to the heart's desire of many a designer. Surprising, is it not, the oodles of ways to show I ♥ Hearts and I ♥ Charms?

In 1956, when screen idol
Robert Wagner proposed
to 18-year old Natalie Wood,
her heart charm bracelet
stole the limelight
in their engagement photo.
The heart symbol,
as timeless as love itself,
will never, ever lose its charm.

A day of sorrow is longer than a month of **joy**.

While you breathe, you **hope**.

It may be those who do most, **dream** most.

Wherever you go, go with all your **heart**.

Good Fortune Foretold
in the
Talking Teardrops

Love is blind. Friendship closes its eyes.

Laugh, and the world laughs with you.
-- Snore and you sleep alone

*"The memory of all that.
No, no! They can't take
that away from me."*

–Ira Gershwin

From your old treasures, new charms!

There may be a special piece of jewelry waiting to happen tucked within your own drawers. Look through your things with a fresh eye and charms in mind and you may be surprised. A vintage family memento, like a foreign coin, a locket, a commemorative medal or a collection of small treasures can make a fabulous transformation into a lucky and very meaningful charm or charms. A jeweler can help you attach it to a bracelet or a chain, or you may wish to have a professional embellish it further. If you are artistic, or have friends who are, look through your miscellaneous baubles for charm material. An orphan earring, loose bead, broken bits can be recycled into some extraordinary and creative charms! You can add new elements, like beads and spacers, to mix with the found items. It's like having a walking scrapbook of your life!

"We fell in love in a holding pattern over the Denver airport. The full moon was *right there* out the porthole. Ever since, all my jewelry revolves around the moon and stars and celestial motifs!" As this couple's romantic meeting shows, any motif can become a personal love token.

There is nothing more romantic than a heart, many would claim. Ahhh, but what about the keys to the heart? Here, there's one to every chamber and then some, each design working like a charm. Don't forget the padlock!

« I kissed a lot of frogs, but I finally got the prince! »

Anything can be a love token when you're smitten.

Couples invent their own symbols of love and devotion.

Better than texting...better than scrapbooking...it's charming! A great new way to make a new BFF, keep the old...one in silver and the other in gold.

Sometimes the inspiration is ...inspirational! For these spiritual charms, also worn as pendants as the case may be, the artistry is inspired, too. How we pray, in any culture, any religion, is a beautiful thing, and many of these exquisite symbols of faith throughout antiquity are highly prized, collected and bestowed.

An old proverb reads, "Crosses are ladders that lead to heaven." How exquisite the rungs inspired by various cultural traditions and modern designers' visions. Opposite: the perfectly perpendicular Taos cross charms with their rustic Spanish mission influence.

> **“Reason is our soul's left hand, Faith her right.”**
>
> –John Donne

"If you judge people,

You have no time to love them."

Mother Teresa

The sale of these special bracelets to individuals and for fundraising events has benefited The Breast Cancer Research Association founded by Evelyn Lauder, Susan G. Komen for the Cure, City of Hope, The Salk Institute, The American Heart Association, Seeds of Peace, Women for Women International, USA Cares, Action Against Hunger and Charity: Water (clean water in Kenya).

just
charms

cause
with a purpose

C harms are for sharing. They give encouragement, pass along strength and speak when words fail. In a "we'll get through this together" spirit, they bond families and friends. Nor are lending comfort and giving something pretty mutually exclusive. There is a special elegance to an ornate personal talisman with a deeper purpose--one that might help mend a broken heart or speed a cure.

ee the pyramids along the Nile. Watch the sunrise on a tropic isle…all from the vantage point of your bracelet. See the market in Old Algiers, send me photographs and souvenirs, or better yet, a shiny charm to keep the travel memories alive. Fly the ocean in a silver plane, see the jungle when it's wet with rain. Singing along yet? The vacations memorialized in song are also recalled in miniature versions of the people-places-things you've seen around the world. Maybe it's a collection of souvenir foreign coins dangling from a bracelet in a fabulous jingly jangly way. Little postcards in their own way, the charms summon fond remembrances on call. Think of them as photo albums on a chain. When hanging en masse, the travel charms become a permanent record of all your magical mystery tours, once-in-a-lifetime sojourns and adventurous escapes to far-flung soils.

*"I know Martin Eden's
gonna be proud of me,
Many before me
have been called by the sea...."*
—Tom Waits

56

Tides may turn in fashion, but the lure of the sea is a constant amongst charm aficionados. Consider the staying power of a seashell charm. Once prized as amulets by many cultures, and used as currency by some native peoples, the shell conjures beachcomber memories and sandpail by-the-sea vacations. Ocean-themed charms take a maritime tack for cruising, motoring or sailing the seven seas. As they say, all hands on deck!

go west!

With the birth of Route 66, and the rise of the interstate highway system, everyone revved up for the great American road trip. Vacationers watched for Burma Shave signs, blue plate specials and curio shops to lasso a new cowboy charm. From the totems to turquoise, the rodeo to the Alamo, Big Sky Country to the Gold Country, the Rockies to the Ranchos, the lure of the frontier souvenir lives on.

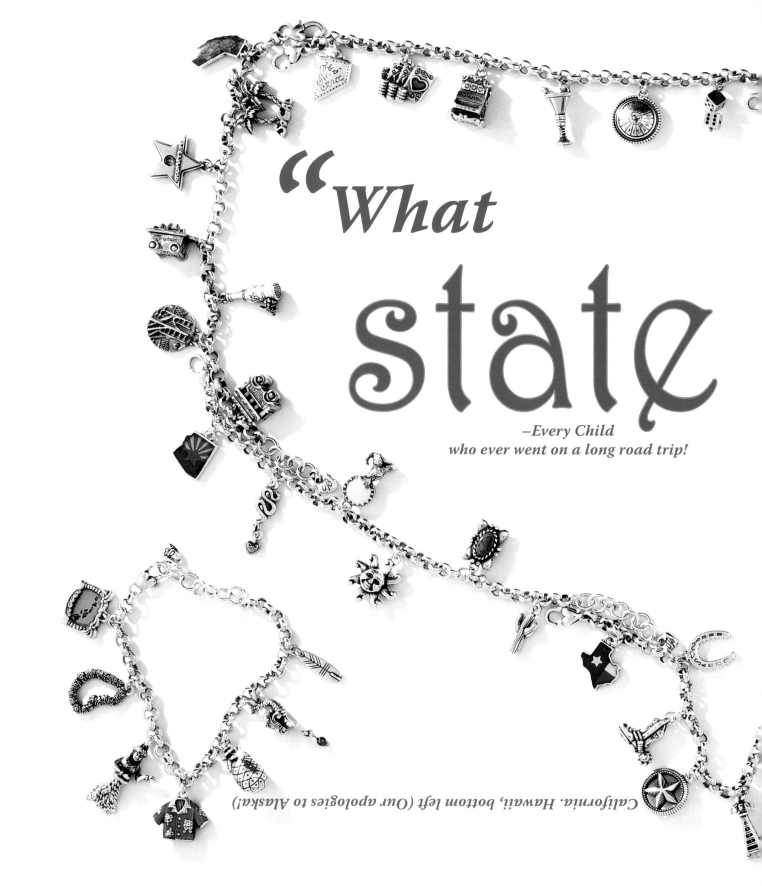

"What state

–Every Child
who ever went on a long road trip!

California, Hawaii, bottom left (Our apologies to Alaska!)

are we in?"

*Can you guess the state
by the charms on each bracelet?
The answers are below...*

Stuff a sock. Hang on a tiny tree. Trim a present. Host a charm exchange. Slip inside a holiday card. Give to teacher. Set by table placecards.

Dangle from mistletoe. Surprise an old friend. Imagine all the things you can do with a single holiday charm or a handful and some shiny links.

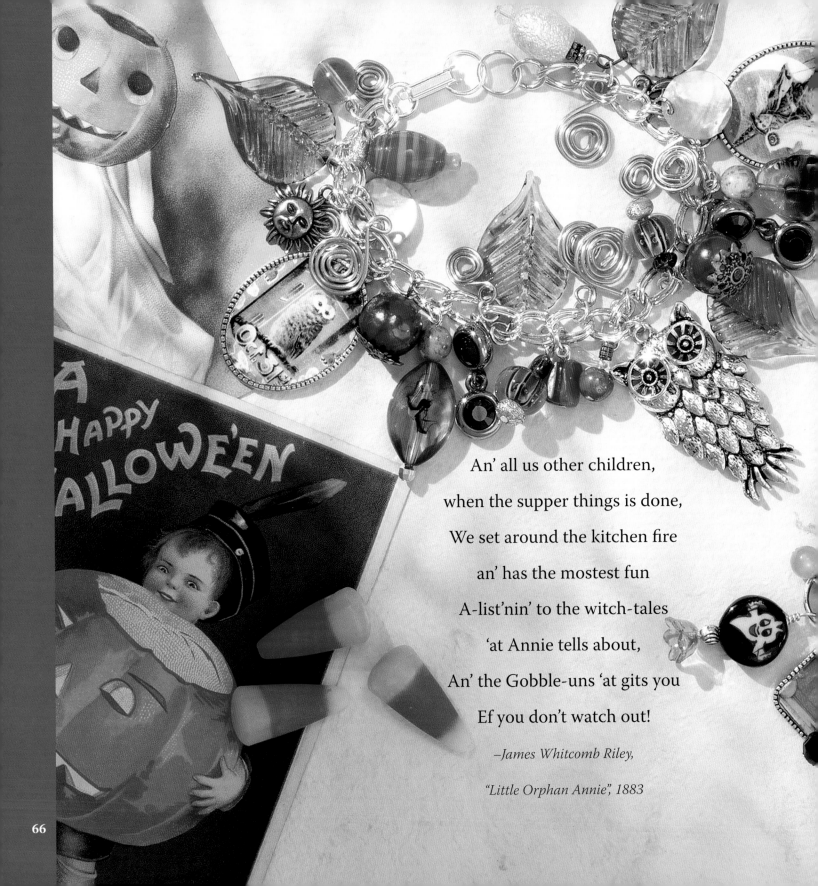

An' all us other children,

when the supper things is done,

We set around the kitchen fire

an' has the mostest fun

A-list'nin' to the witch-tales

'at Annie tells about,

An' the Gobble-uns 'at gits you

Ef you don't watch out!

–James Whitcomb Riley,

"Little Orphan Annie", 1883

what inspires the designer?

Few factors offer more creative inspiration than one's roots. When Maryam, a soft-spoken designer of jewelry and accessories, shows the antique inkwells she has collected in her native Persia, you sense the excitement in her voice. It's easy to become engrossed in the romance of these pieces dating to the Qajar Dynasty of the 18th and 19th centuries. Who were they made for? Whose hands have they passed through? One of the inkwells shows a royal heritage. On its lid, the king's seal and a compass. Another is ruby and turquoise-encrusted. While slipping the silver or brass wells inside a papier-mache qulamdan (pen holder) for use, Maryam tells how everyday objects of this period were all inexplicably lavish and ornate. One of these inkwell patterns became the inspiration for her "Persian Garden" pierced and etched jewelry designs.

heritage

CHILDREN

Ricky 2-14-54

Marilyn 7-11-58

Judy 11-24-61

Jeffrey 9-22-64

GRANDCHILDREN

Tina 1-12-76

Matthew 7-21-82

Sean 10-3-86

Rachel 10-3-86

Jeff Jr. 3-5-89

Ethan 11-9-91

◄ If this charm could tell tales, what adventures it would relay. The story would begin in Finland, and speak of its original purpose as a coin. It would relay its travels in this gentleman's pocket on a long journey to the New World. But that was years ago, long before his daughter took it to the jeweler to have it framed with gold and stones. Now it is a precious keepsake, worn often around the neck of a granddaughter who remembers the trip with her mother to make the charm, a significant moment in her life's journey as well. Family charms are the most precious of all, often divulging secrets and sometimes solving mysteries of the past for the family historian.

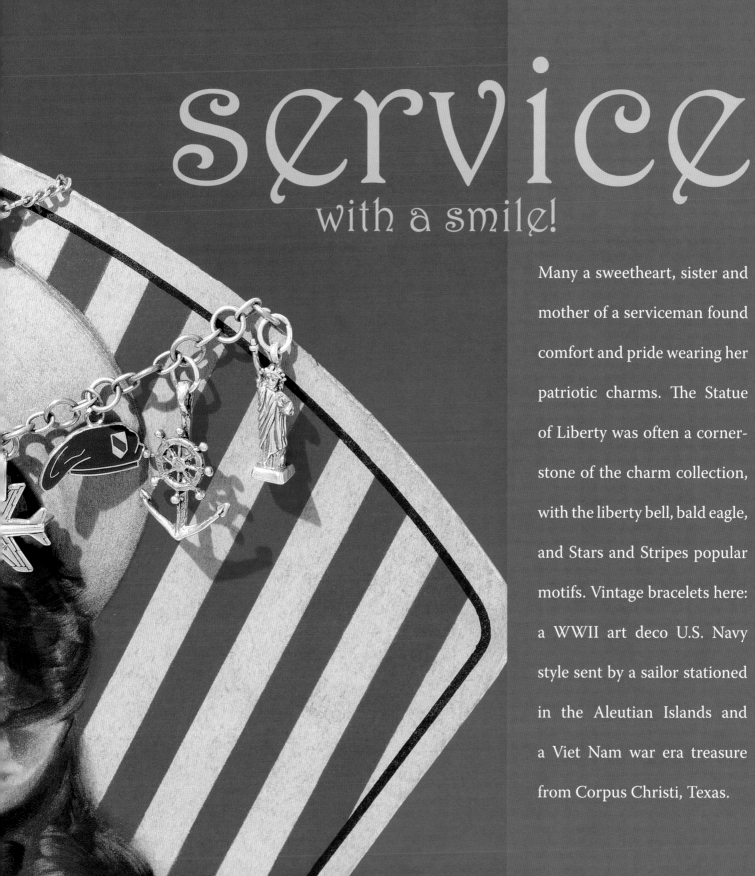

service
with a smile!

Many a sweetheart, sister and mother of a serviceman found comfort and pride wearing her patriotic charms. The Statue of Liberty was often a cornerstone of the charm collection, with the liberty bell, bald eagle, and Stars and Stripes popular motifs. Vintage bracelets here: a WWII art deco U.S. Navy style sent by a sailor stationed in the Aleutian Islands and a Viet Nam war era treasure from Corpus Christi, Texas.

what inspires the designer?

Just a child when she was first surprised by the ad displaying her rare and pretty name, Mavis had no idea how it would inspire her for years to come. Already artistically inclined, the woman who became a jewelry designer was mesmerized by the art deco graphics and the gracefulness in the lines of the fragrance bottles. She started a collection of the posters and lovely period design scent bottles then and there, and looks to it for ideas today. Always one to imbue meaningful thoughts and poetic images into her design work, Mavis sees this inspiration as life's journey coming full circle. Look how the lyrical movements in the current piece compare with yesterday's arts.

personal

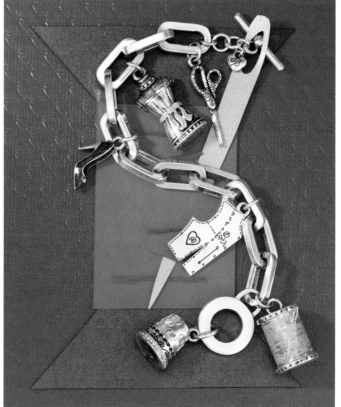

passions

Maybe you're a skier, a seamstress, a magician or somebody's mommy. Or do you adore animals,

collect teapots, play tennis or the piano every chance you get? The activities that make us

individual make some of the most charming theme bracelets of the "pre-fab" sort. Dangling with

charms representing personal passions, these are the ID bracelets of the 21st century.

If one happens to attract the attention of a like-minded soul ("Oh, you play tennis too?")

it could make an introduction or be a matchmaker. Charm bracelets are flirtatious by nature.

*What inspires
the wearer?
Loyalty.
To their school,
their pet, their
hometown.*

Cheerleading takes to the wrist. The idea: lucky charms will win one for the home team. The imagination gets free reign with themes going beyond school spirit and sports arena.

Texting…here's the way to do it with charms. This message was sent to a teacher who wears charms from A to Z in perfect alphabetical order. Her students get a lesson in creativity as a bonus. Using spacers between the letters, the charms do the talking, or the LOL-ing as the case may be. Spelling out a name, a favorite quote, a team cheer or even a random alphabet soup with charms turns a necklace or bracelet into a good read. Anagram lovers can mix 'em up and keep everyone guessing.

*Back on its golden hinges
The gate of Memory swings,
And my heart goes into the garden
And walks with the olden things.*
—Ella Wheeler Wilcox

pop culture

Sure, we'll still love them when they're sixty-four. Hey, Jude, you won't let the Fab Four down... The music, the movies, the toons, the events of the times influence our lives, all the way down to our jewelry. On occasion, the jewelry inspires our pop culture in return. That's the charming thing about it.

edia darlings tell all! These charms-of-the-times chime in with their own brand of tinkling ring tones...or save a place between the pages. (Charms at work!) They are also communicators in their own right, apt to spark a conversation by offering the first "Hello!" to the stranger in the train station, the bleachers or the library stacks.

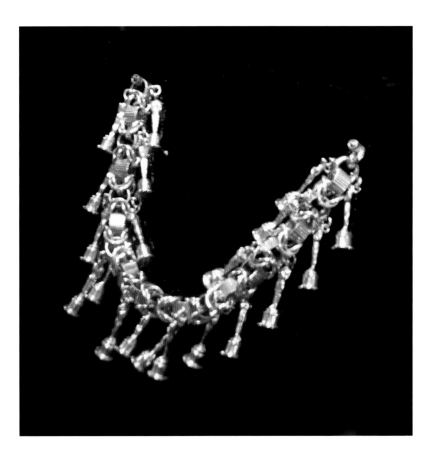

Walt Disney amassed far more Ꭺcademy Ꭺwards® during his long career than an average trophy cabinet might hold, 22 in all. Walt had the statuettes miniaturized as gold charm mementos and hung on this bracelet. Mrs. Disney had the honors of showing it off to the world. When she wore it, all the Oscars® were in a state of "suspended animation"!

©Academy of Motion Picture Arts and Sciences®
Academy Awards, Oscar, and the Oscar design mark are the trademark and service marks, and the Oscar statuette the copyrighted property of the Academy of Motion Picture Arts and Sciences.

"Let the chips fall where they may," Marlene Dietrich might have said, as she played her hand in a charm bracelet of poker chips. A gift from Frank Sinatra, the actual bracelet is now in a museum in Berlin, Germany, her native country. The two mid-century screen stars shared a love for poker, and each starred in casino movies. Dietrich was in "The Monte Carlo Story" of 1957, promoted as the "Land of the high stakes and low-cut gowns"; Sinatra in "The Man with the Golden Arm", 1956.

Collectors pay a pretty penny for these gumball machine prizes. Back in the day of penny candy, Sputnik bubblegum and these early versions of vending machines, metallic-glow plastic charms were the "it" thing with kids of all ages.

" Sugar, Oh, Honey Honey. You are my candy girl, and you got me wanting you. "

– The Archies, 1969

How did they do that?

Efforts to unearth a prehistoric charm bracelet led to Bedrock, the Flintstones turf where there was a lot of yabba dabba doing over this fimo clay design starring in "Viva Rock Vegas" (Universal Pictures 2000 release). Modeled after these contemporary charms (the magic of movies at work!) by costume designer Robert Turturice, the custom-made bracelet rocked on the wrist of the stone-age choreographer character Jason Kravits during the Rockettes opening scene at the Tardust Hotel. "The minute he put it on, it came alive," says Turturice.

Here is how one prominent jewelry company creates their detailed, delicate charms in the original sketch-and-model method. The artist and artisan still have a hand in the labor-intensive process of making each miniature masterpiece.

Step One: The sketch. Using a two-dimensional format, the artist conceives and draws the design from every angle for the three-dimensional end product.

Step Two: The model. Working from the drawings, artisans who have learned their craft through traditional methods carefully hand-carve the designs in wood, first in a large scale, then again in miniature, capturing every detail.

Step Three: The mold. Steel molds are created from the wood models.

Step Four: The finishing. Charms are then cast and silverplated. In some cases the charms are color-enameled using molten glass powder, a time-consuming, multi-step process requiring patience and artful skill.

Step Five: The decoration. The artist's design determines the trims, in many instances the finest Swarovski crystals.

M

arry Me, the proposal bracelet, is a true story. Romantics, get out your tissue! One smitten guy stopped into a specialty store to have a sales associate help him compose this charmer before he popped the question. Presumably his intended said yes…and one day soon he'll be back creating a MOM picture bracelet. Moral of the story, when in doubt, just spell it out.

It usually begins with a bracelet.

Obsessions with self-expression, charm by charm, bracelet by bracelet, goes with the territory of being a girl. "The same but different"—her prerogative. Best friends forever collect together—her motto. At the tender age of 6, one shopper regularly shows up at the charm department each time she gets her grades. Good report cards equal a new charm. This time it's a unicorn. There's a dolphin already set aside. She arranges her own charms on the bracelet with a very discriminating eye.

How to start a "Great Beginnings" bracelet for Baby (that will last a lifetime!)

She came into the world the most charming little bundle. Celebrate with her birthstone charm. As  she splashes the bubbles in her bath, give her a rubber ducky charm. Holidays roll around, Santa will make an appearance—on her new bracelet. With three charms, it's already a collection. Choose baby shoes when she takes her first step, an animal to remember her first plush toy. On her first birthday, add the number 1. (Just seen: a 16-year-old with a fanciful bracelet of jangly numbers collected on each birthday of her life.) For every milestone, a memento. Since Baby must not wear charms until it is safe for her to do so, proud Mama can don them in the meantime. By the time Baby turns Schoolgirl, she'll have a very special piece of jewelry of her own.

"I am part of all that I have met," wrote poet Alfred Lord Tennyson. That's the idea with this "This is your Life!" bracelet presented to Liane at her milestone birthday party. Each friend contributed a charm representing a shared adventure, experience or memory. As each tiny gift was opened and the individual stories told, it served as a party icebreaker. This is the collective result, an instant biography.

Big Ben, a shared memory of a year spent in London.

Prompted by a trip to the Soviet Union, the cross tells of a mutual fascination with the last Czar and his family.

Nine-year-old budding actor's pick: the chair for when Liane directs him in a theatre production one day.

Just among friends, the speculation— are the aliens really "out there"?

From one night owl to another. What a hoot.

One night the new roommates let the spaghetti burn. Neighbors phoned the fire department.

liane's

100

Some day: a fantasy escape across old Route 66, via a vintage Airstream.

A best friend gets philosophical with the iceberg representing things to be done that loom larger and nearer the more one puts them off.

The lizard...from the desert vacations spent prone at the poolside with friends, just "skimming the surface."

The biggest laugh: an ear of corn triggering a funny memory of a favorite Broadway show tune, "Jerry's Got My Corn".

surprise

Do your own "This is Your Life" charm gift party for birthdays, Silver or Golden Anniversary, Mother's Day, Graduation or Bridal Shower.

♥ Invite party guests to participate in the group gift, explaining the concept of the collective charm bracelet.

♥ Specify silver or gold color charms.

♥ Have someone choose the link bracelet.

♥ Suggest charm stores in the local area, or websites to shop.

♥ Assemble, leaving space, if you wish for more memories.

♥ Have a jeweler solder the jump rings for security.

*U*ptown, downtown.
Street chic, hot boutique. All girl,
very guy. Charms are the new
tools of self expression, crossing
every boundary and letting every
man, woman and child simply be
their charming selves.

“*I loathe narcissism, but I approve vanity.*”

— Diana Vreeland

Soaring on the popularity charts with the mega stars: charm necklaces and bracelets. Pop diva Mariah Carey wears her charms in concert, letting the little tinkle of the metal be part of the music. She even titled an album "Charmbracelet." Penelope Cruz, Madonna, and Sharon Stone (shown clockwise from top left) are seen here dangling amulets of every sort.

inspired

Sometimes charms aren't jewelry at all.
They're just charming pattern motifs for other favorite
articles in a person's life. Piggybacking on the trend,
charms turn up on an Estee Lauder see-through
cosmetic case. Fashion designer Monique Lhuillier
is inspired by charms, too, on the china pattern she
created for Royal Doulton. It's rimmed with a delicate
chain motif with a lucky shamrock charm.

Charms make a quick zip around a datebook or an organizer.

Earrings dangle charms. By land: a cluster of leaves; by sea, shell motifs.

Instantly festive: sweaters or jackets given holiday zipper pulls.

Smart ID idea. Wineglass charms attach to the stems, each charm unique for each guest.

The most glamorous of exits, dangling charms on your heels in haute couture fashion.

The heart with a magnetic attraction shows off one's love of shoes—from the refrigerator door, perhaps?

Sign with love, using the pen and its charm.

Chatelaine-inspired pin
with charms and links to the past.

There's a charmed life ahead for
Baby in an embellished frame.

Charms to keep a golfer at the top of his/her
game, worn on the belt keeper
or the key fob.

The Queen Mom and her little Princess
tie their sneakers alike with royal charms.

*Charms have jumped
their links, and
sometimes the body,
to attach themselves
to our daily lives every
which way. Some are
ancient ideas made new
again, others borne of
necessity, ingenuity or
mere whimsy.*

This isn't The End.
Like the never-ending circle
of the bracelet, the charm story is
infinite. A keeper of memories, charm
jewelry is alive, forever growing and going
along with you on life's journey. As long as
we have hopes and dreams, we will go on
making, wearing and carrying charms
for fun, for luck and for love.

Acknowledgments

Abundant thanks to Jerry Kohl, Founder of Brighton;
without his genius and generosity this book
would not have been possible.

Project Editor: Lori McFadden
          www.lorimcfadden.com
Writer: Phyllis Hansen
          www.phyllishansen.com
Creative Contributors: Beth Barror, Tom Clancy,
Maryam Nassirbegli, Mavis Peterson, Peggy Reed.

All still photography by Brian Goodman and
Public Works Studio, unless noted below.
All model photography by Kevin Foley
unless noted below.

Photos from Corbis on page 7, Sandro Vannini/Corbis;
page 9, Gunn & Stewart/Bettmann/Corbis; page 19, Bettmann/
Corbis; page 20, Bettmann/Corbis; page 31, Bettmann/Corbis;
page 35, Bettmann/Corbis; page 88, Seth Joel/Corbis; page 90,
Louis K. Meisel Gallery, Inc./Corbis; pages 104, David
Bergman/Corbis; page 105, Frank Trapper/Corbis/Sygma.

First published in 2009 in hardcover in
the United States of America by Brighton, Inc.
14022 Nelson Avenue, City of Industry, CA 91746
www.brighton.com

Library of Congress Control Number: 2008941751

ISBN-978-1-932802-51-1